Pro-action in Defence of the Jewish State

G.M. Ben-Nathan

www.proactionjewishstate.com

THE ENGAGEMENT

www.the-engagement.org

G.M. Ben-Nathan
website: www.proactionjewishstate.com
email: gmbn@proactionjewishstate.com
written under the auspices of
The Engagement
www.the-engagement.org
PO Box 2412, Rehovot 76123, Israel

First edition published by The Engagement

A catalogue record of this booklet is
available from the British Library.

ISBN: 978-1-910301-16-6

Printed and bound in Great Britain by
Lightning Source UK Ltd,
Chapter House, Pitfield, Kiln Farm,
Milton Keynes MK11 3LW

Pro-action in Defence of the Jewish State

Contents

Contents

Contents

Acknowledgements

First and foremost to Tsvi Misinai in Rehovot, Israel. His activism in the field in pursuit of 'Re-engagement' is an inspiration as is also his '*credo*' 'Brother shall not lift up Sword against Brother'. May this booklet, especially Part III, aid and abet his mission.

Thanks also to Elon Jarden in Netanya. Elon is simultaneously a historian and philosopher – an intellectual giant. His is the mind behind the whole concept of Re-engagement. I am grateful for the hours of time he has bestowed upon me.

Thanks, too, to Professor Joseph (Yossi) Ben-Dak. It is flattering that a man of his great eminence should wish to contribute a foreword. I am honoured and grateful.

Thanks also to many UK friends and colleagues who, wittingly or unwittingly, have served as sounding-boards for this or that theory. This very much includes my close associate and friend Tanya Warburg and my dear wife Margaret. Their support has been vital and their caution, often necessary, most salutary.

Finally, I would like to thank Martin Noble (mart@copyedit.co.uk) for all his help in editing and designing this book.

Geoffrey Ben-Nathan
London, August 2014

Foreword

by Professor Joseph (Yossi) Ben Dak

In his *Descriptio Imperii Moslemici*, the great tenth-century historiographer Al Muqaddasi sets out treatment given to Jews when he comments: 'in Khazaria, sheep honey and Jews exist in large quantities'. This disrespectful remark was noted by Arthur Koestler in his famous book on the Khazars, *The Thirteenth Tribe*. It was ever thus, both before the tenth century and right up until today. Reference to Jews has often been disparaging, unfair and prejudiced. Whoever behaves like this – thankfully not everyone – seems to get away with it. Jewish genius has alternatively been advantaged and then discarded without praise or recognition.

No-one is more acutely aware of this than the author of this booklet. He offers his readers the chance to get to grips with the phenomenon, to find out where those who defame Judaism and the Jewish people are coming from – and, importantly, *why?* Of course, these days, the Jewish state, Israel, takes the flak. It wears the mantle, Ben-Nathan asserts, of 'pariah' status formerly borne by diaspora Jews. Today Israel is denigrated by the world media, shallow commentators, religious leaders, ignorant politicians and a host of Jews who fail to pass the test of *l'dor va-dor* – Jews not in a generational chain of Jewish continuity but who are unfortunately its end link.

Despite the onslaught, we try to maintain our values. We do not act as 'they' do. We resist the beguiling temptation 'to be like they are'. Our enemies are not destroyed. They so easily could be and could have been. Instead, they are left to attack us again and again and again. They are supported by an increasingly hostile world practising Boycott, Disinvestment and Sanctions (BDS) against our Jewish state. This is simply the clear and loud voice of hatred, fuelled in many cases by ignorance. This is also the voice of those in thrall to dominating and tyrannical ideologies – political, religious and secular. It is also the voice of passive minds easily led.

I met Geoffrey Ben-Nathan for the first time in June 2014 in Netanya when a mutual friend brought us together. He had read this booklet in draft and recommended it, and I read it too. I received so many new ideas, so much new understanding. For example, the importance of using the preposition 're-' and how it immediately resuscitates a vital Biblical connection; and the observation about the so-called self-hating Jew, mentioned above. All this was new to me and it adds up.

He told me he had studied Anthropology as a student: anthropology, he said, is 'the deepest me'. Personally, I am not so sure about this: his Jewishness also runs deep and his passion for finding out the deepest '*why*' of everything is very Jewish. It led to his first book in 2008 on juvenile delinquency in which he called for a rite of passage to help youngsters make the transition from childhood to adolescence. As far as verbal attacks on Israel are concerned, Ben-Nathan believes each attack has its own very specific 'right answer'. He says he has tested them in battle in his occasional UK Arab media appearances.

What will the reader get out of all this? First, I think, a degree of self-confidence. The reader can perhaps for the first time move from defensiveness to informed attack. He or she will have at his or her disposal a large body of factual information for use in the and fro of debate. Here in Israel, in my opinion, many Israeli spokesmen fail: they lack the know-how to use and interpret their facts. Secondly, Ben-Nathan educates us to 'know our enemy'. He slaughters quite a few holy cows that have been allowed to dwell in all kinds of feeding grounds for far too long. He provides critical knowledge for choosing your response strategy.

Finally, the third part of Ben-Nathan's booklet considers the Palestinians and their identity, which is a very sensitive topic. Some observers, with similar commitment to the author may argue that involvement in this subject is a little early. My own position is simple: when one deals with the relationship between Palestinians and Israelis, all too often we begin and end talking about conflict and security. When the Israeli Council for Peace and Security pronounces on this theme, it asks: 'What political solutions can survive?' 'What security initiatives make sense?' 'Has there been a proper sanction to stop terror?' All these bear the stamp of the stick, the hammer, the weapon. Not enough is articulated by way of the carrot.

What can be done to improve the life of the *fellahin* living in our midst? What planning can be pursued together? What 'superordinate goals' – following the 'peace thinking' of the late Muzafer Sherif (1906–1988), the great Turkish American social psychologist can be developed? It is my belief that when such thoughts and ideas come to dominate our thinking in spite of the difficult terrain in which we seem to gobble up the identity of Arabs as enemies, we will need to have a fresh look at identities.

The author wrote to me recently, complaining that the world's most illustrious statesmen – of this century and the last – have failed to make any headway in solving the Middle East problem. He asked if I thought that if Sherlock Holmes were alive today, *he* could disentangle the Gordian knot that is the Middle East. Ben-Nathan thinks that broadcasting Ben Gurion's and Ben Zvi's views about Palestinian origin could be a Sherlock Holmes masterstroke. Well, he could have another think coming. But hey – wasn't it Ben Gurion who said that to live in the Middle East, you need to believe in miracles?

Factual realities may not be our easiest spectrum to consider but when we say 'we', and we mean both them and us, this set of 'thoughts on

Palestine' that Ben-Nathan has provided is both timely and critical for all of us.

Joseph D. Ben-Dak
Nahariyyah, July 2014

Professor Joseph ('Yossi') Ben-Dak, *PhD, DSc (http://the-engagement.org/?page_id=40) worked for the United Nations Development Programme (UNDP) as Principal Advisor to the UN Secretary General (1991– 97). He has been Professor of Peace Studies and Policy Sciences at the University of Haifa and in Korea and a Professor of Science Policy in Brazil and in Asia. He was the founder of FAIR (Foundation for Arab-Israeli Reconciliation) and is currently Chairman of the Knowledge Planning Corporation (KPC), a strategic multinational think tank helping to provide government departments, military establishments and international corporations with advance strategic thinking and planning towards future goals. He is also Vice Chairman and CSO of Advanced Reconnaissance Corporation; Chairman of Aeronautica Reliance and of Counsel, Mid-Market Securities.*

PART I

FIRST PRINCIPLES

1 Introduction

1.1 Who Am I? What is The Engagement?

Who Am I ? I am a single individual. I attend a small anonymous *ad hoc* group. It meets in London every six weeks or so. We discuss the Jewish state. As Jews, we often agree to disagree. One contact within our group put my name forward to an Iranian TV station. They wanted an apologist for the Jewish state. The broadcasts to the Muslim community that followed are a privilege I cherish. They have afforded the opportunity to formulate these thoughts and ideas.

What is The Engagement? The Engagement[1] is a movement to unite Jew and 'Palestinian' 'Arab'. As of now it is 'a still small cloud'. Its time is yet to come. And it will. Engagement or, better, "Re-" Engagement, is based on the sound scholarship of famous men. Part Three of this Paper refers.

1.2   What Is Our Objective?

Our objective is to defend the Jewish state *pro-*actively.

1.3   What is *Pro-*action?

Sometimes it seems that the world, or some of it, is never more comfortable than when condemning the Jewish people. If it cannot do so directly, it does so through the proxy of the Jewish state. For example, more than fifty per cent of all Resolutions of the United Nations General Assembly are country-specific condemnations of the Jewish state.[2] The record of the United Nations Human Rights Council is even worse.

Exponents of *pro-*action are alert to this. They do more than just react. Refuting this or that malicious allegation is not the limit of their objective. They are pre-emptive. They initiate, they anticipate, and they counter-attack.

What follows is a distillation of our findings which, broadly speaking, are of three types:

1. Recommended 'do's' and 'don'ts', tested 'in battle' so-to-speak

2. Identifying recurring themes that lurk behind attacks on the Jewish state; analysis of these themes

3. Discussion of issues – particularly 'Palestine' and 'The Palestinians'. This discussion is 'food for thought'. This 'food' may be added, or not, as you wish, to your own current thinking on these subjects.

1.4   Who Is This Booklet For?

The booklet is for whoever is involved in defending the Jewish state, be it at a dinner party or in social media, writing or broadcasting. The subject of 'Israel' can come up at any time. As often as not, allegations are made and you need to know how to refute them. You also need to know how to sow doubt in the minds of those listening to you.

2 Preparation and Presentation

2.1 Courtesy and Formality

- Be polite.
- Be formal.
- Address everyone by their title, e.g. 'Dr', 'Professor', 'Your / His Excellency' etc.
- Don't lose your temper – if you lose your temper, you may lose the argument.
- People judge you as much by your demeanour as by what you say.

2.2 Do Your Homework

- Do your homework.
- Be streetwise and clued-up.
- Research topics as best you can.
- Research your hosts and fellow participants.

- Discover the track record of those who are making allegations. They may do so frequently and they may always be critical. If so, they cease to be objective, which becomes an issue in itself.

2.3   Ask Questions

- Ask questions. The question is a very powerful tool. It puts the respondent on the defensive and this may be all you have to do. The rest, if you are lucky, will take care of itself. This applies to *all* encounters, no matter what forum: one-to-one, national media and everything else in between – everybody mentioned in 1.4 above.

- A frequent scenario: the Jewish state is being attacked. You have had to listen to a sustained and perhaps prolonged tirade. At last you are able to intervene. Everyone is expecting you to counter-attack.

- You *don't* counter-attack. You say to your opponent words to the effect:

  'For five (ten, fifteen, thirty whatever) minutes you have been listing the evils of the Jewish state, but what *we* would like to know is what you think the Jewish state should have done / should do in the future?' In other words, put the ball straight back in their court. The effect is often riveting.

- Don't make a long preamble. This is fatal. One sentence, maximum two, is all you should allow yourself.

- Unless you are a principal speaker, people really do not want to hear *your* thoughts.

2.4   Example

A public meeting – one of many – was convened in London to support the Palestinian cause towards the end of 2008 at the time of the inaptly named Operation Cast Lead. The principal speaker spent her time haranguing the Jewish state. She accused it of war crimes and much other nefarious behaviour.

A questioner was moved to ask a question of the type described above: 'So can you kindly tell *us* how you think the Jewish army *should* be behaving?'

'Well, if I were an Israeli soldier,' she said, 'I'd go out into the field with all my colleagues and hug Hamas with open arms. I'd throw my arms round them and welcome them.' She recommended all kinds of bonhomie.

You could detect a perceptible *frisson* of discomfort at the sheer naivety and impracticality of this advice – advice proffered in a hall full of her own supporters.

One small question, short and well-timed. That is all it takes.

3 More Preliminaries: Says and Don't Says

3.1 Say 'The Jewish State' – Don't Say 'Israel'

Your listeners may not realise that Israel is a *Jewish* state. But opponents know this and they trade on it, so they say 'Israel' all the time. By doing so, they demonise and de-legitimise. And they get away with it. They find this less easy to do if *you* say 'the Jewish state'. Only a few people are innately Jew-hating; most people know that Jews are not demons. It does not ring true.

So keep saying 'Jewish state' and you may note your opponent/s become discernibly uncomfortable. You successfully undermine their attempt to demonise. To those who are hostile, or might be hostile, we say 'the Jewish state'; to those we know are 'friends', 'Israel' is fine.

3.2 Say 'Jewish Nationalism' – Don't Say 'Zionism'

The terms 'Zionist' / 'Zionism' are also demonised. They are equated with 'ogres' and 'monsters'. Extreme opponents talk of 'Zionist Nazis'.

Use the expanded definition: 'Jewish nationalist' and/or 'Jewish nationalism'. They reflect the true meaning.

Once again, using a substitute term undermines the attempt to demonise.

3.3 Say 'Hatred of Jewish People' – Don't Say 'Anti-Semitism'[4]

The word anti-semitism has lost its pejorative stigma. It sounds almost innocuous. If you want to show you mean what you are saying, say: 'Jew-bullying', 'Jew-hatred', 'hatred of all Jews' – perhaps preceded by the word 'innate'.

3.4 Use the Prefix 'Re'

- Say '*re*-establishment of the Jewish state'; don't just say: 'establishment'.

- Say '*re*-settlements'; don't say 'settlements'.

- Say similarly '*re*-settlers'; don't say 'settlers'.

- Say '*re*-occupation'; don't say occupation.

- We *do* say '*re*-turn – but with the accent on the *second* syllable!

Using the prefix 're' stops people in their tracks. They can only infer you are referring back to ancient times. This is exactly the point. You *are*.

3.5 Say 'Arabic-speaking People in the Jewish State' – Don't Say Arabs and/or Palestinians

Why?

Because most (not all) Arabic-speakers in the Jewish state are **not** Arab. Language and ethnicity are not coterminous. Are all speakers of English in the world British? No, they are not.

This acknowledges a new reality. Arabic-speaking Christians in the town of Nazareth have publicly disavowed Arab identity.[5] Muslims may follow suit. More on this later.

3.6 Say (Where Appropriate) 'Ceasefire Line' – Don't Say: 'Green Line'

Ceasefire line is correct. The 'Green' line is a ceasefire line from 1948. It is *not* a border. Israel has negotiated borders only with Egypt and Jordan.

3.7 Say 'Judea and Samaria' – Don't Say 'West Bank'

Judea and Samaria are historic parts of the Land of Israel. So are their inhabitants. Israelite Samaritans from the Tribes of Ephraim and Manasseh have dwelt uninterruptedly in Samaria for over three thousand years. They are there to this day in Shechem (Nablus) and Mt. Gerizim. They observe the precepts of the Five Books of Moses (The Torah). These are written in the proto-Hebrew script of the Hebrew language.[6]

4 *Pro*-action and *Re*-action to Recurring Themes

4.1 Introduction

Exponents of *pro*-active defence of the Jewish state (and other causes too) must learn to distinguish between 'surface allegation' and 'sub-surface motivation'. The one rarely has anything to do with the other. Of the two, for the *pro*-active defender, sub-surface motivation is by far the more important. This is often a focus for counter-attack.

Defenders of the Jewish state have hitherto concentrated on *re*-acting to surface allegations. They seem to assume these allegations are made in good faith. Whatever the case, they seem to feel it sufficient to do little more than refute them.

Whilst *re*-active refutation is necessary, it should not be the be-all and end-all. More must be done. 'Sub-surface' motivation must now be addressed.

4.2   Theme 1:   Diversion Strategy

Proclaimed statement: *'We must **all** of us first work together against Fascist Israel and the dastardly way it treats the poor Palestinians. It's **treacherous** to worry about anything else. Only after victory can we work on our own affairs.'*

Real intention: To divert opposition. General Galtieri[7] is a classic example: intense anger towards his regime changed literally overnight into unadulterated adulation.

***Pro*-action response:** Show that you know what is really going on. Expose diversion strategy for what it is – diversion strategy.

Let your audience know: the perpetrator has received no threat.

- Outrage has been largely manufactured.
- No-one has any real issue with the Jewish state.

Expose corruption and mismanagement in the hostile leader. Proclaim that corruption and mismanagement are what they are really trying to hide.

The Jewish state has constantly been the victim of diversion strategy. Iran is practising it today. Iran's real objective is to develop nuclear weapons. Destruction of Israel is the excuse. Iran's neighbours are not fooled.

Victim's response: A victim state must take 'diversion strategy' very seriously. Dictators become prisoners of their own propaganda. Unintended wars are started. The victim must be prepared.

4.3   Theme 2: 'Soft-Touch' Targets

Surface expression: Outrage and often activism. Outrage and activism are proportional to the degree that the selected target is perceived to re-act. 'Soft-touch' targets are usually what their name implies.

Sub-surface motivation: To look and feel politically good, fashionably good too, in one's chosen milieu.

Comment: The trick is to be selective. It is vital to select regimes pre-calculated not to react harshly; or preferably not to react at all. The Jewish state was thought to be a prime soft-touch target. Democracies, generally, are soft-touch targets. Brutal regimes are usually studiously avoided.

Occasionally, activists miscalculate. Greenpeace miscalculated in October 2013. Their activists tried to board a Russian ship. The Russians did not play the game. Activists were arrested, accused of 'piracy' (fifteen years in prison) and 'hooliganism' (seven years). It was all a nasty shock. Russia 'overreacted', so Greenpeace said.

In the end, 29 activists spent three months in prison. Greenpeace may reconsider returning to the Arctic. Meanwhile, Russian ships continue to explore for oil there.

*Pro-*action response: Portray 'soft-touch' in terms of one-sidedness and selectivity. Proclaim a failure to engage with totalitarian regimes: North Korea, China, Zimbabwe, etc.; challenge activists to address these too; accuse activists of chasing 'easy victories' by only going for the 'soft-touches'.

4.4   Theme 3: Replacement Theology

Definition: Shorthand term for one religion (Judaism) being replaced by another (Christianity or Islam) on the grounds that it (Judaism) has been superseded by new revelation (the advent of a Messiah, Jesus Christ, or the Prophet Mohammed).

Surface expression: A blistering attack on Jewish morality. It used to be on Jews directly (deicide, well-poisoning, blood libel). The Holocaust (temporarily) put paid to this. Now, the Jewish state, 'Israel', is substitute.

Israel is demonised in every way. It can do no right. Its response to its every predicament is grossly wrong. Good points are overlooked – as are the bad points of those to whom the Jewish state is obliged to react.

Attack is on Jews in the Jewish state rather than Judaism (though circumcision and ritual-slaughter have recently re-surfaced).

Sub-surface motivation: Replacement theology reinforces self-reassurance, self-belief and self-justification. Those that practise it feel self-satisfied.

Accusers occupy moral high ground at the expense of those whom they accuse – often the Jewish state that pointedly does not.

4.4.1 Replacement Theology – Christianity

4.4.1.1 *Introduction*

In today's world we have to be careful. The *Jewish* state receives enormous and very welcome support from Christian evangelicals all over the world. We do not wish to offend them. So, defence of the *Jewish* state must only be in response to criticism from each individual Christian source – not Christianity as a whole.

4.4.1.2 *Case Example*

St James's Church, an Anglican church, is located in London's Piccadilly. Over Christmas 2013–14, at great (donated) expense, the church erected in its forecourt a facsimile of the West Bank security barrier. The church claimed to be supporting 'the peaceful Palestinian principle of "beautiful resistance"'.[8] That may be so. But the church was also impugning the moral integrity of the Government of the Jewish state.

Surface *re*-action: The venture was a great success. Everyone was talking about oppression by the Jewish state of Arabic-speaking minorities within it. The only morality in question was the behaviour of the Jewish state and those supporting it.

Sub-surface *pro*-action: Very little. The Church's agenda was sustained.

What might have been said then and in the future:

(a)   *The Jewish state*

The Church need be told politely but firmly: the God of the Hebrew Bible is alive and well. Jews look for no substitute. He does not need replacement. He is active in today's world. Many Jews, non-Jews too, believe the Jewish state could not have been re-created without His active participation. They also believe He oversees their actions. They do their best to relate to Him as best they can.

The leadership of the Jewish state runs the state to the best of its abilities with humane Jewish values. It needs no lessons in morality from the Church or anyone else.

Most Jews want the Jewish state to be 'a light unto the nations'.[9] In many respects, it is. It acts in the most moral way it can in all the many predicaments it has been forced to face.

(b)   *The Security Barrier*

One such predicament was the 2002–05 *intifada*. In this period, three thousand Muslims in the Land of Israel lost their lives – as did one thousand Jews. The Security Barrier was built. It has done its job. It is still doing it – for Muslim and Jew alike. Since its erection, casualties for *both* have plummeted.[10]

The clergy of St James's Church in London criticise. Anyone can and everyone does. But in the hotspot, what would they do? It would be nice to know!

4.4.2   Replacement Theology – Muslims and Islam

It is not difficult to address the Muslim community. What needs to be said is clear and simple: Jews read the Qur'an. The Qur'an, Suras 5:21 and 17:104 and elsewhere, makes it quite clear[11] that the Holy Land has been 'written' (i.e. ascribed) to the Jewish People. You so often refer to this Holy Land as 'the Zionist entity'. But this 'entity' is quite clearly written to the Jewish people in the Qur'an itself.

In this circumstance we ask all Muslims, especially Muslim leaders, Imams and Sheikhs, to think again: to reconsider whether the return of the Jewish People to the Holy Land and the re-establishment of the *Jewish* state there, is not, as Muslims have seemed so sure, **against** the Will of Allah, but, much more, **by** His Will.

Allah has had over one hundred years to kill off Jewish nationalism (Zionism). Allah, the Almighty, does not, of course, need this time. He could do it in seconds. His Will is supreme. But Allah has obviously been pleased with *Jewish* return and resettlement of the Land of Israel. What else is there to infer?

Muslims may be surprised to learn that we Jews pray to Allah. He is Almighty God to our common ancestor, Ibrahim/Abraham. And we believe that Allah has been answering these prayers.

4.4.3   Final Comment

The re-establishment of the Jewish state in 1948 has shaken both Christianity and Islam to their very roots. It was simply not meant to happen. It was not in the script. Eternal exile was the fate of a literally Godforsaken Jewish people. Re-establishment of Jewish sovereign independence was hoped to be a temporary aberration.

History must soon correct itself. Jewish sovereign independence is an embarrassment. And some branches in the 'daughter religions' work towards the restoration of the status quo ante. They will not give up.

4.5   Attacks from Extreme Left, Extreme Right and Atheists

Surface Expression: Moral outrage expressed selectively at the plight of Arabic-speakers in the Jewish state. The Jewish state, 'Israel', is the nominal target; Jews and Judaism are the real objective.

Sub-surface motivation: One cannot know for certain. Possibly, as with Replacement Theology, fury that Jews stubbornly cling to Jewish values. In doing so, by default, they reject *other* philosophies. Extreme Left and Extreme Right extol a supremacist state. Jews extol the institution of the family. On this basis alone, they are natural antagonists.

Pro-action: Meet them head on. Elaborate the polarity between state and family. We make no apology; 'state' has failed time and time again; family has not. We believe this to be true for all human beings – not just Jews.

PART II

CONTEMPORARY ISSUES

Introduction to Part II

The subjects dealt with in Part II (Chapters 5–8) are all 'surface-issues'. Beneath them lie 'sub-surface' issues, which are referred to above. Consider which they might be.

5 Boycott, Divestment and Sanctions (BDS)

We've seen it all before. In the 1930s – in Nazi Germany.

You could take a lenient approach. You *could* say: 'You're not Nazis, of course. But where else are you advocating BDS? Is it just against the *Jewish* state? Why? Are you being hypocritical?'

Or you could, if you feel the occasion merits it, be more aggressive: 'You're not Nazis of course. But actually it's not *quite* clear, BDS-wise, *how* you differ. How *do* you differ? Have you got plans to patrol Jewish businesses?

6   Jews against Jewish Nationalism (Zionism) and the Jewish State (So-called Self-hating Jews)

6.1   Introduction

*'And you shall teach **your children** diligently...'*

Thus runs the fourth verse of Judaism's most recited prayer, the *Shema*.   Jewish survival, as in other cultures, depends on continuity.   No (Jewish) children, no continuity.

There are Jewish childless couples; there are many couples whose children, or some of them, have married out; there are plenty of Jews who have not married at all.   No-one suggests for a moment that they turn into Jews against Judaism, Jews or the Jewish state – *chas vechalila* (Hebrew: God forbid!). Far from it! Judaism, Jewry and the Jewish state all flourish with their ardent support.

A small minority, though, seem to turn in upon themselves and their fellow Jews.   Some are even citizens of the Jewish state.   They call for reduction in the size of the Jewish state (small as it is); and, in some cases, for its total demise.

Who knows what is going on in their minds? But one interpretation is: 'if I have no Jewish future, I don't want one for anyone'.

Some of these Jews have reached high office and great prominence. They do inestimable harm. Those looking for a quick 'take' on the situation can reasonably be assumed to think: 'Well, if this is what a Jew is saying of his own people, he (or she) *must* have a point.'

6.2   Dealing with Jewish Activists

As always, first refute the surface issue(s) as best you can. This surface issue may be an expression of effusive concern for Arabic-speaking Muslims in and outside the Jewish state ('Palestinians').

6.3   Counter Attack

Obviously the matter of personal status is very delicate. One must be very sure of one's ground before addressing it. Nevertheless, the 'continuity' phenomenon embraces many so-called self-hating Jews.

When sure of your ground. Ask about personal status: 'Are those with no Jewish future trying to confound those that have? Is not the Jewish state an essential crucible nurturing one generation into another? Is this not a wonderful thing? Would you have it any other way? Minority status might be the way for you. But do you advocate it for all your Jewish brothers and sisters? After the experience of the Holocaust, are you serious?'

7 The Hebrew Language – a Key *Pro*-active Aid

Hebrew, the language of the (Hebrew) Bible, fits into the Semitic languages of the Middle East like a hand fits into a glove. (Actually, it's the other way round. The Semitic languages fit into Hebrew. Hebrew pre-dates almost all of today's spoken Semitic languages). Yet those who speak Hebrew *in situ* are often denounced as 'colonisers'.

Did the British reintroduce Bantu when they colonised Southern Africa? Did the French reintroduce Wolof or Mandinko when they colonised West Africa? Did the Spanish colonise South America speaking its native languages? No, they did not! The very thought is ludicrous. They imposed their own languages on one and all.

Not so, Hebrew. The Jewish state is its homeland. It is where it belongs – as do those who speak it. We are talking of *re*-colonisation – not colonisation.

Use Hebrew (you don't need to speak it yourself) as a *pro*-active tool. Publicly ask detractors where they think Hebrew comes from. How do they think the Jewish people got hold of it? (Did they 'steal' it?) How have they managed to keep it so long? Your audience may get some very entertaining answers.

The fact is the possession of the Hebrew language is the key connector between the Jewish people and the Land of Israel or the Holy Land (as it is sometimes called). Its importance cannot be overstated.

8 Judaism and Jewish Nationalism

There are 'universals' in Judaism: the Ten Commandments and a host of moral laws. Many Jews see Judaism as speaking to the world. It certainly does. But it is also a very 'particular' religion. In its 'particularity' it speaks only to its adherents – just Jews.

Nowhere does it speak just to Jews more than on the question of land. On this issue, the Hebrew Bible is the foundation for Jewish Nationalism (Zionism). Behave in accordance with Biblical precepts – universal and particular – and you will be allowed to live in the Biblical homeland; misbehave, then expulsion or rule by others will result.

'Exile' and 'return' are pre-ordained in the Torah – the Five Books of Moses. For (just one) example, see the fifth book, Deuteronomy, chapter 29:

> 23. *Even all the nations shall say:'Wherefore have The Lord done thus unto this land? What meaneth the heat of this great anger?'*

24. Then men shall say: 'Because they forsook the Covenant of the Lord...'

27. And the Lord rooted them out of their land in anger, and in wrath, and in great indignation, and cast them in to another land, as it is this day.

As much as expulsion is pre-ordained, so also is return. Take the next chapter, chapter 30 (*emphasis added*):

1. And it shall come to pass, when all these things are upon thee, the blessing and the curse, which I have set before thee, and thou shalt bethink thyself among all the nations whither the Lord thy God hath driven thee,

2. and shalt return unto the Lord thy God, and hearken to His voice....

*3. that then the Lord thy God **will turn thy captivity**, and have compassion upon thee, and **will return and gather thee** from all the peoples, whither the Lord thy God have scattered thee.*

The certainty of eventual return to the land is intensively reinforced in the additional books of the Hebrew Bible – the Prophets and the Writings. The Rabbis continue the theme. They brilliantly kept the scattered, world-wide Jewish community together from CE 135 to CE 1948. They do so to this day. They codified Jewish Law. They wrote the prayers for the synagogue. Naturally, as Rabbis, they saw return to Zion in spiritual terms.

Just a cursory glance at an orthodox Hebrew prayer book will show how very many prayers the Rabbis devised for the restoration of Zion. They craved deliverance from exile – deliverance perhaps led by The Almighty Himself (*emphasis added*):

> *O sound the great horn* [the ram's horn, the shofar] *of our freedom: and raise the banner to gather our exiles, and* **gather us** *speedily together from the four corners of the earth,* **into our own land***. Blessed art Thou,* **O Lord!** **who wilt gather** *the outcasts of thy people Israel.*

This is one of the nineteen blessings of the *amidah*. The prayer is still recited by every orthodox Jew three times a day. The theme is constant.

As it happens, spiritual Zionists lost out. Prayer has not in itself been enough. Not-so-religious, political activist Zionism won the day. But this, here, is by the by. Here, we have a limited objective. It is merely to state:

The Middle East conflict is often debated in exclusively political terms. But the *pro*-active defender should know, and he should be able to tell his audience, that Judaism itself is a strong 'sub-surface' component. It is the 'elephant in the room' – not mentioned or invoked nearly as much as it should be. Judaism *is* Jewish Nationalism (Zionism). The two are inextricably linked. Neither survives without the other.

PART III

THE JEWISH STATE AND THE 'PALESTINIANS'

9   Thoughts on 'Palestine'

The Romans renamed Judea/Samaria 'Palestine' circa 135 CE. In doing so, they reacted to Jews who were forever in rebellion against them. The intention was to banish Jews and Judaism from the land. The name 'Palestine' has stuck.

The Israeli author, Tsvi Misinai, asks an interesting question.[12] What would the residents living in Judea over the centuries have been called if the Romans had not made this change? Today's 'Palestinians' would be called, he asserts, 'Judeans' who are 'Muslim by faith'.

Misinai also poses the question:[13] is there any other dispute on Earth where two peoples are fighting for every square inch of precisely the same territory, each as sole and legitimate owner in exclusion of the other?

How can this be? There are only three possibilities:

1.   both peoples are wrong – neither has a legitimate claim. This can be ruled out.

2.   One is right and the other is wrong – in which case, which one? And why? Or

3.   Both are right. How can this be? Only, if *both are the **same** people*.

David Ben Gurion and Yitzhak Ben Zvi both believed this to be so. To be precise, they proved the *fellahin* (the Arabic-speaking farmers on the hills), in particular, to be of Jewish origin.

The pioneer Israel Belkind wrote an essay:[14] 'Where are the Ten Tribes?'

There is no necessity, he said, to go on a wild-goose chase (not, his words) looking for them here, there and everywhere. They are all hiding in plain view in the hills of the Land of Israel – in Judea and Samaria and beyond.

10 'The Palestinians'

This paper's view on 'Palestine' and the 'Palestinians' derives from the finding of David Ben Gurion[15] and Yitzhak Ben Zvi.[16] Despite their pre-eminence, their view is virtually unknown. It has therefore played no role whatsoever in the debate that has raged these many decades. What is more, their finding is game-changing. It is truly revolutionary. So what did they say?

Ben Gurion and Ben Zvi researched the *fellahin* – the Arabic-speaking farming community settled in the Land of Israel. They found that they are *overwhelmingly Jewish in origin*. Their settlement long pre-dates the Arab conquest of 636 CE:

> and there is no doubt whatsoever that in their veins flows much Jewish blood – blood of those same Jewish farmers, people of the Land (*amei ha-aretz*), who chose in hard times to renounce their religion only that they might not be uprooted from their land.
>
> David Ben Gurion: *Clarification on the Origin of the Fellahin.*[17]

Figure 1 *Book co-authored by Yitzhak Ben Zvi and David Ben Gurion. Title translates as: The Land of Yisrael – Past and Present. First published in Yiddish 1918; translated to Hebrew 1980.*

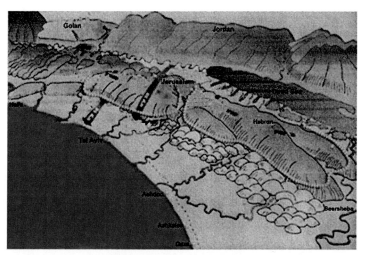

Figure 2 Relief map of Israel.

פלחים יהודים בפקיעין

*Figure 3   Jews of the Upper Galilee village of Peki'in. Uniquely,
Jews have lived here resisting pressure to convert to Islam. Jewish
fellahin (Arabic-speaking hill farmers) – a culture unchanged from
Temple times. 1932 photo in the 1980 Hebrew edition of Ben Gurion
and Ben Zvi's book; reproduced here by kind permission of the Ben
Zvi Institute, Jerusalem.*

63

Modern science upholds these findings. Many Arabic-speakers in the Jewish state share DNA with Ashkenazi Eastern European Jews.

Bedouin who live in the Jewish state are genuinely Arab. They are, though, a minority among the Arabic-speaking community.

You might think that Jews, Arabic-speakers and non-Jews alike would be very pleased to hear of the Jewish-*fellahin* connection.

You could be very *wrong*!

Why?

The Middle East dispute (call it what you will) has lasted for decades. People have adopted positions. They are entrenched in support of their positions. They are by now in a 'comfort zone'. Few want change. You attempt it at your peril!

Furthermore, many positions are financially supported. Money funds hundreds of organisations dedicated to this or that aspect of the problem. The annual budget for UNWRA (United Nations Relief and Works Agency) is just short of a *billion* dollars. Money means jobs. They cannot be threatened. In this scenario, nothing threatens jobs more than 'peace'.

One cannot be too cynical in matters political – 'We want Peace' often means precisely the opposite. Too much is invested by *both* sides in the status quo for any real change ('peace') to be welcome.

So why are you being advised to tread where angels fear to go?

1. Because it is the right thing to do. The time is ripe for Ben Gurion's and Ben Zvi's finding to be put on the agenda. It militates against bloodshed.

2. *Pro*-active defenders of the Jewish state can tap into a new and rich vein of advocacy – namely, that Jews and most 'Palestinians' are not two quite separate different peoples. They need not forever be mortal enemies.

3. The 'Palestinian' people are a means to an end. They are regarded as an Achilles heel of the Jewish state. The very last thing pro-'Palestinian' organisations want to hear is that many 'Palestinians' are historically part of the People of Israel. Worse that these people may

one day return, not as converts but, like Christians in Nazareth, citizens who now want to be loyal to the Jewish state. The Christians of Nazareth are now calling upon their youth to enlist in the Israeli Defence Force (IDF).

Such a message sabotages, demolishes even, blind support for 'Palestinians'. This is powerful and positive *pro*-active counter-attack.

11 'Palestinians' – Further Comment

Two more questions to answer: firstly, *why* has Ben Gurion's and Ben Zvi's finding remained 'hidden' for so long? One can only speculate: perhaps because it was written in Hebrew. This has only recently been translated into English. It is not yet widely available; secondly, the Hebrew text is 'embedded' in a large work; thirdly, the finding was offered as (literally) matter-of-fact scholarship – nothing particularly revolutionary at the time.

However, Ben Gurion and Ben Zvi were major figures in the early history of the Jewish state. They had power and influence. Maybe they found their finding (in the 1920s and '30s and beyond) was so far away from the reality of implacable hostility that it could not be practically pursued.

If this was so, some may feel that nothing has changed.

The second question is usually a simple *'so what?'* Arabic-speaking people might very well have once been Jewish. But they are obviously not now.

So *why* go on about it? Just accept that they now are who they are.

What to say to this? Yes, this is true. In this world, it is not unknown for brother to fight brother – even to the death. But surely, in this case, in particular, *both* sides should at least *know* they are brothers. It might make a difference. It might alter attitudes. It *ought* to alter attitudes.

Having said this, one or both sides may prefer to perpetuate the status quo.

Mutual enmity has become a *modus vivendi*. One or both sides may want the enmity to continue. If that is the case, little can be done. At least one tried.

12 'Palestinian' Refugees

The subject of refugees is another purported Achilles heel of the Jewish state. Numbers have burgeoned. Inflation is the name of the game. No one knows the true figure. Those that crave the demise of the Jewish state as a *Jewish state* regard the return of refugees as a trump card. They could be mistaken.

Pro-active defenders of the Jewish state should familiarise themselves with the work of Elon Jarden[18] and Tsvi Misinai.[19] They simplify the problem. They focus upon those with roots in the Land and those with no roots in the Land. They note that in the War of Independence (the war which secured the independence of the Jewish state in 1948) those with roots in the Land stayed put – hence, the Arabic-speaking population which constitutes one-fifth of the Jewish state. Those with no roots in the Land did not stay put. They left.

Who are those with roots in the Land?

Those who dwell in the hill country of the Jewish state; those also who dwell in hill country beyond the 1948 eastern ceasefire line. This is the territory that left Jordanian control in 1967. Some call it 'the West Bank'.

Who were those with *no* roots in the Land? Who were those who left?

Jarden and Misinai both state that those who left were economic migrants – people who came temporarily to support Jewish nationalist enterprise. Much of this was conducted on the plains bordering the Mediterranean. The authors also state that the 'surnames' of these migrants – those who are now refugees - emphasise their foreign origin.

These people have had a most unfortunate fate. They have become fossilised as refugees. They have certainly been used as political pawns – not least by those with sharp axes to grind against the Jewish state, for example, adherents to replacement theology. The United Nations Relief and Works Agency (UNWRA) has largely been funded by Christian countries. Presumably it was they who *uniquely* decided to allow refugee-status to be inherited from generation to generation. This is something which has never occurred before or since anywhere in the world.

Why has this been allowed? One can only speculate: many Jews see it as a reflection of Jew-hatred. So great is hostility for renewed sovereign Jewish independence that everything that can be done must be done to bring about its eventual demise. How better than to perpetuate the 'running sore' of the 1948 refugees and to carry them into a thousandth generation?

The refugees are said to live in refugee 'camps'. The idea of temporary tent cities comes to mind – perpetuated from 1948! Nothing could be further from the truth. The 'camps' are permanent structures. Living conditions are indistinguishable from surroundings areas. Everything in the terminology is malevolently designed to convey the idea of a 'continuing open wound'.

There are now third- and fourth-generation 'refugees'. Original refugees from 1948 are dying out. Meanwhile, the desire of donors to provide the largesse remains unabated.

Thus the life of the 'refugee' may not be so bad. UNWRA funding has been truly munificent. Its 2013 budget as mentioned is just short of a *billion* dollars. Some individual 'refugees' are alleged to be in receipt of several stipends. Deaths among 'refugees', apparently, go unrecorded. Payments continue. Who would not think twice about relinquishing such bounty?

It remains the fact that in any final settlement these poor people have never truly been refugees. They deserve, however, considerable compensation. Nevertheless, return must be to their real homes of origin.

13 Once Muslim Land – Always Muslim Land: Not So

13.1 Introduction

The Muslim sage Taqi ad-Din Achmad ibn-Taymiyyah (1263–1328) is credited with the *fatwa* (legal opinion) calling for eternal struggle (*jihad*) to oust non-Muslims who gain control of Muslims and Muslim land.[20]

Jewish control of the Holy Land in 1948 is a case in point. For nearly 1300 years, it had been under Muslim suzerainty. Muslims are thus duty-bound to regain supremacy.

But *did* ibn Taymiyyah really call for eternal *jihad*? It seems he did not.

Muslims citizens of the town of Mardin, South-Eastern Turkey, fell under non-Muslim Mongol control. Ibn Taymiyyah was asked to deliberate. What should they do? His *fatwa* was unequivocal: as long as the non-Muslim ruler protects Muslim lives and Muslim property, they need not worry.

So how has ibn Taymiyyah come to be cited as the source for eternal *jihad* ?

It all seems to be the result of a terrible mistake, a typographical error! Tens of thousands of lives have been lost, are still being lost, it would seem, to this typographical error!

What was the typographical error and when did it first occur?

It first occurred in 1909. In this year ibn Taymiyyah's collected *fatawa* were first printed. The printer, Fraj Allah al-Kirdi, reproduced ibn Taymiyyah's original word, *yu'amal,* as *yuqatal,* meaning not that the non-Muslim leader should be treated with (*yu'amal*) but rather than the non-Muslim leader should be fought with (*yuqatal*). The error was unnoticed. It has gone on being reproduced until recently. The corrupted text has appeared in English, French and other languages.

Incalculable damage has been done. Militant Islam uses the *fatwa's* wording as prime justification. It, allegedly, explicitly inspires al-Qaeda.

But no-one is more devastated by Islamic militancy than the Islamic world itself. Establishment Islam felt the need to expose this printing error.

13.2 The New Mardin Declaration (June 2010)

Thus it was that a conference was held in June 2010 in ibn Taymiyyah's home town (Mardin). The Conference was attended by many of today's most eminent Muslim scholars. Among them Emeritus Professor of Riyadh's al-Imam University, Sheikh Abd al-Wahhab al-Turayi, and former Mauritanian Government Minister, Sheikh Abdullah Bin Bayyih, who chaired the Conference. Muslim theologians and academics from Bosnia, India, Iran, Indonesia, Kuwait, Morocco, Turkey, Saudi Arabia and Yemen also participated.

The two-day Conference issued the 'New Mardin Declaration'. This restored ibn Taymiyyah's *fatwa* to its original and very peaceful intention. The typographical error has been publicly exposed. As long as non-Muslim rulers treat their Muslim subjects with proper respect, there is no imperative whatsoever to fight with them – over land or anything else.

Reference was made to ibn Taymiyyah's only surviving manuscript. This of course has the correct uncorrupted text. It is lodged in the Zahiriyyah library in Damascus.

What publicity will the Declaration receive?

Will it undermine *jihadi* militancy?

So far, unfortunately, the answer is a resounding 'No!' But *pro*-active defenders of the Jewish state must be aware of the New Mardin Declaration and all its implications.

14 Conclusion

Specific techniques and precise lines to take have been recommended. Many have been tested in public meetings and broadcasts. There is evidence that they are effective.

What is the evidence?

The evidence is that hostile allegations successfully refuted result in their being quickly and quietly dropped. Debate moves on. The *pro*-active defender has neutralised the assault and hopefully turned the tables.

The *pro*-active defender has also here been given 'food' for thought – especially on the subject of Arabic-speaking people within the Jewish state.

The line this paper takes about 'Palestine' and 'the Palestinians' is new. It has been tested in one broadcast. It seemed to be successful. The Muslim presenter was a little taken aback. It represents hope for the future; it also represents reality. The move made by 'Palestinian' Christians in Nazareth has been publicly welcomed by Israel's Prime Minister of the day, Mr Netanyahu. So do not feel, in taking this line, you are in cloud-cuckoo land. You are not.

Jews are in the majority in the Jewish state. Understandably, they wish this to remain so. Jews are only too well aware of their vulnerability in minority status. Feeling of self and family security can alter overnight.[21] However, the Jewish state with its Jewish majority is a plural state. It embodies citizens of other religions and none.

Muslim Arabic-speakers beyond the ceasefire line might one day wish to resuscitate their blood relationship with the Jewish people. The Israeli Tsvi Misinai, who works for re-engagement,[22] has laid down conditions. His conditions are not easy to meet. Were they to eventuate, he certainly does not feel numerical superiority of Jews in the Jewish state would in any way be overturned.

One thing is certain, the greater the number of truly loyal citizens, the stronger and more permanent, the Jewish state.

References

1. Website: www.the-engagement.org is in three languages: Arabic, Hebrew and English (with subtitles).

2. http://www.jcrcboston.org/focus/support/resources/un-bias-against-israel.html

3. http://www.israelnationalnews.com/News/News.aspx/176991#.U2iNt8pOXIU

4. http://www.britannica.com/EBchecked/topic/27646/anti-Semitism

5. http://www.youtube.com/watch?v=2gMNYPR48gQ&feature=youtu.be

6. http://www.israelite-samaritans.com/

7. http://en.wikipedia.org/wiki/Leopoldo_Galtieri

8. http://www.theguardian.com/commentisfree/2014/jan/02/bethlehem-unwrapped-not-taking-sides-israel-security-wall

9. Isaiah 42:6.

10. http://en.wikipedia.org/wiki/Israeli_West_Bank_barrier

11. Sheikh Dr. Muhammad Al-Hussaini (2009) Claims to the Holy Land – 'The Qur'an's Covenant with the Jewish People'. *Middle East Quarterly*, Fall 2009. The article quotes extensively from one of Islam's greatest commentators: Abu Ja'far Muhammad ibn Jarir at-Tabari (838-923). At-Tabari confirms Sura 5:21. He ascribes the Holy Land with the widest borders (Exodus 23:33).

12. 'Brother Shall Not Lift Sword Against Brother' (Tsvi Misinai (2008) *The Roots and Solution to the Problem in the Holy Land*. Liad Publishing, 3rd edition, March 2008, p. 310).

13. Ibid., p. 259.

14. Israel Belkind (1928) 'Where are the Ten Tribes?' re-published by the Hermon Press, Tel Aviv, 1969.

15. David Ben Gurion co-authored with Yitzhak Ben Zvi (1918, 1980) *The Land of Israel – Past and Present*, First published 1918 in Yiddish. Translated to Hebrew and published by the Ben Zvi Institute, 1980. See 'The Origin of the *Fellahin*, pp. 195–206.

16. Yitzhak Ben Zvi (1937) *The Writings of Yitzhak Ben Zvi – Part 5, 'The Populations of Our Land'*. Chapter 3, Origin of the *Fellahin*, pp. 135–149 (Hebrew), Mitzpeh Publishing 1937.

17. David Ben Gurion (1969) *Regarding the Origins of the* Fellahin (Hebrew) Hermon Publishers, Tel Aviv.

18. Elon Jarden (2013) *Land of Mountains and Plains: The Demographic History of the Land of Israel*, Liad Publishing (Hebrew). Available on the web in English as: 'Between the Mountains and the Plains.' *In the Eye of the Storm* (Hebrew) Liad Publishing, August 2013.

19. See n. 12 above. Tsvi Misinai (2012) *The Engagement – The Roots and Solution to the Problem of the Land* of Israel. Liad Publishing (Hebrew). http://the-engagement.org/

20.   http://www.thenews.com.pk/Todays-News-9-241183-The-new-Mardin-declaration

21. http://www.bbc.co.uk/news/world-europe-27088183

22. See n. 12 above, pp. 324–7.

About the author

G.M. Ben-Nathan, born London 1944, has made appearances on UK-based Muslim media defending the Jewish state. The ideas outlined in this booklet derive from research for and experience from these programmes.

website: www.proactionjewishstate.com
email: gmbn@proactionjewishstate.com

How to order

For complete details of the latest UK letter and postal charges, please check the website at: www.proactionjewishstate.com

Paperback copies of this booklet are available from the author for **£4.99** each plus:

- **£1.50** postage and packing to the UK (1 booklet)
- **£2.00** postage and packing to the UK (2–3 booklets)
- **£3.00** postage and packing to the UK (4–5 booklets)
- **£3.50** postage and packing to the UK (6–7 booklets)
- **£6.00** postage and packing to the UK (8–15 booklets)
- **£5.00** postage and packing to countries outside UK (1 booklet)
- **£8.00** postage and packing to countries outside UK (2–3 booklets)
- **£11.00** postage and packing to countries outside UK (4–5 booklets)
- **£14.00** postage and packing to countries outside UK (6–7 booklets)
- **£25.00** postage and packing to countries outside UK (8–15 booklets)

How to make payment:

- *By post:*

  Payment by cheque to:

  G.M. Ben Nathan
  2 South Ealing Road
  London W5 4BY
  United Kingdom

  Please write or type in BLOCK CAPITALS all addresses, i.e. your address for receipt and (if applicable) address/es to which you want the book/s sent.

  *Please allow **ten** days for dispatch.*

- *Online via Paypal at*

  www.proactionjewishstate.com

  *Please allow **ten** days for dispatch.*

  Kindle ebook version

  Available from Amazon: **£2:99**

For all enquiries:

Please email **gmbn@proactionjewishstate.com** or write to author at address above.

Lightning Source UK Ltd.
Milton Keynes UK
UKOW03f0832150814

236958UK00001B/2/P